Copyright

This is a work of ingredients. Any resemblance to actual ingredients, or locales is entirely coincidental.

Table of Contents

Table of Contents

Table of Contents

Overnight Oats

Preparation Time: 8 min

Serving: 1

6

INGREDIENTS

- ½ tsp. maple syrup
- Pinch of sea salt
- ½ cup whole rolled oats
- ½ cup almond milk
- Desired toppings from above

DIRECTIONS

1. Combine the oats, almond or coconut milk, maple syrup, and salt in a small jar. Stir and chill overnight.
2. In the morning, scoop the oats into a bowl stir in more almond or coconut milk, if desired, for consistency. Top with desired toppings.
3. Alternatively, you can assemble the overnight oats in jars with the toppings the night before for a grab-and-go breakfast.

Overnight Chocolate Chia Seed Pudding

 Preparation Time: 20 min

 Serving: 4

INGREDIENTS

- ¼ cup cacao powder
- 1 pinch sea salt
- ½ tsp. vanilla extract
- 1 ½ cups light coconut milk
- ½ cup chia seeds
- 3-5 tbsp. maple syrup
- ½ tsp. the ground cinnamon, optional

DIRECTIONS

1. In a small-size mixing bowl, whisk together cacao powder (sift first to remove clumps), maple syrup, ground cinnamon, salt, and vanilla. Then mix in a bit of amount of dairy-free milk until paste forms. Then blend in the remaining dairy-free milk until smooth.
2. Whisk in the chia seeds one more time to mix. Then cover and chill overnight, or at least 3-5 hours (until a pudding-like consistency is produced). Additionally, after 30-45 minutes in the refrigerator, give the mixture one extra whisk/stir.
3. Leftovers keep covered in the refrigerator for 4-5 days but are best when fresh. If desired, serve chilled, topped with fruit, granola, or coconut whipped cream.

Coconut & banana pancakes

Preparation Time: 25 min

Serving: 10

INGREDIENTS

- Vegetable oil for frying
- 2 tsp. baking powder
- 3 tbsp. golden caster sugar
- 2 bananas, thinly sliced
- 2 passion fruits, flesh scooped out
- 150g plain flour
- 400ml can coconut milk, shaken well

DIRECTIONS

1. Mix the flour and baking powder into a mixing bowl; add 2 tablespoons sugar and a teaspoon of salt. In a dish, pour the coconut milk and whisk to include any separated fat, then measure out 300ml into a jug. Slowly incorporate the milk into the flour mixture until a smooth batter forms or whizz everything in a blender.
2. Brush a shallow frying pan or flat skillet with oil and heat. 2 tbsp batter per pancake, cooking two at a time - any more will make flipping them harder. Incorporate 4-5 banana slices into each pancake and cook until bubbles form on the surface and the edges seem dry. They will be a little extra delicate than based pancakes, so carefully flip them over and cook for an additional minute. Repeat to create different 8-10 pancakes.
3. Meanwhile, combine the remaining coconut milk and sugar in a small saucepan. Simmer, adding a touch of salt until the mixture reaches the consistency of single cream. As a sauce for the pancakes, add some passion fruit seeds on top.

Vegan breakfast muffins

Preparation Time: 50 min

Serving: 12

INGREDIENTS

- 2 tbsp. grapeseed oil
- 160g plain flour
- 1 tsp. baking powder
- 250ml sweetened soy milk
- 3 tbsp. nut butter
- 4 tbsp. demerara sugar
- 150g muesli mix
- 50g light brown soft sugar
- 1 apple, peeled and grated
- 50g pecans, chilled

DIRECTIONS

1. Preheat oven range to 200 degrees Celsius/180 degrees celsius fan/gas 6. Using muffin liners, line a muffin tray and set it aside. Combine 100g muesli, light brown sugar, flour, and baking powder in a bowl. Combine the milk, apple, oil, and 2 tbsp nut butter; stir into the dry ingredients. Distribute evenly among the cases. Spoon the remaining muesli over the muffins, along with the demerara sugar, remaining nut butter, and pecans.
2. Bake for 30 minutes or till the muffins have risen and become brown. Keeps for 2-3 days in a freezer or one month in the freezer. Before serving, reheat in the oven.

Vegan French toast

Preparation Time: 42 min

Serving: 4

INGREDIENTS

- 2 tbsp. gram flour
- 2 tbsp. ground almonds
- 3 tbsp. maple syrup
- 200ml oat milk or rice milk
- 1 tbsp. golden caster sugar
- 1 tsp. vanilla extract
- 6 slices of thick white bread
- Grapeseed oil for frying
- 150g blueberries
- 2 tsp. cinnamon
- Icing sugar for dusting

DIRECTIONS

1. In a standard saucepan, gently heat the maple syrup and blueberries until the berries begin to pop and release their juices, then remove them from the pan. Whisk together the flour, almonds, cinnamon, milk, and vanilla extract in a shallow basin.
2. In a frying pan, heat a small-size amount of oil. Soak a slice of bread into the milk mixture, shaking off excess, and cook on both sides until the bread browns and crisps around the edges. Warm the pieces in a low oven while you finish cooking the remainder. Serve with a spoonful of blueberries and a dusting of icing sugar.

Chia pudding

Preparation Time: 6 min

Serving: 1

16

INGREDIENTS

- 2 tbsp. chia seeds
- 2 tsp. maple syrup, + a drizzle to serve
- Mango, to serve
- 125ml oat milk

DIRECTIONS

1. Mix the chia seeds, milk, and 2 tsp maple syrup in a jar or bowl. At least overnight, cover and chill for at least 8 hours.
2. When it's time to serve, add fruit and maple syrup.

Kiwi fruit smoothie

Preparation Time: 5 min

Serving: 3

INGREDIENTS

- 500ml pineapple juice
- 1 banana, sliced
- 3 peeled kiwi fruit
- 1 mango, peeled and chopped

DIRECTIONS

1. Put all elements in a blender and blitz until smooth, then pour into 2 tall glasses.

Pistachio & cardamom butter

Preparation Time: 25 min

Serving: 1 jar

20

INGREDIENTS

- 400g pistachio nut kernels
- 1 tbsp. maple syrup
- 2-3 tsp. groundnut oil
- 10 cardamom pods
- ½ tsp. sea salt flakes

DIRECTIONS

1. Cardamom pods have seeds inside that you can remove. Make a fine powder out of them by grinding them in a pestle and mortar. Make a fine powder out of them by crushing them in a pestle and mortar.
2. Add the nuts to a food processor with cardamom, maple syrup, and salt. Process until the nuts are very smooth. Blend for about 7 to 8 minutes until the soft nut butter is leftover. Then, add a little bit of oil and mix again.

Orange & mint salad

Preparation Time: 15 min

Serving: 4

22

INGREDIENTS

- 4 oranges
- Bunch mint, leaves chopped, + a few left wholes
- 1 tbsp. rose syrup or rosewater
- 12 soft dates, sliced lengthways

DIRECTIONS

1. Peel then segment the oranges, removing the white pith. Place any juices in a bowl, add the dates, chopped mint, and rose syrup and toss gently. Divide between 4 dessert bowls, scatter on the mint leaves, and serve.

Three-grain porridge

Preparation Time: 10 min

Serving: 18

INGREDIENTS

- 300g spelled flakes
- 300g barley flakes
- 300g oatmeal
- Agave nectar and sliced strawberries, optional

DIRECTIONS

1. Working in batches, toast the oatmeal, spelled flakes, and barley in a large, dry frying pan for 5 mins until golden, then leave to cool and store in an airtight container.
2. When you want to eat the porridge, mix 50g of the mix with 300ml of milk or water in a saucepan. Cook for about 5 minutes, stirring now and then. If you want, you can add honey and strawberries to the top if you're going to (optional). Keep it for 6 months.

Black beans & avocado on toast

Preparation Time: 33 min

Serving: 4

INGREDIENTS

- 4 tbsp. olive oil
- 2 garlic cloves, crushed
- 270g cherry tomatoes, quartered
- 1 red or white onion, finely chopped
- 2 x 400g cans black beans, drained
- Bunch coriander, chopped
- 4 slices bread
- 1 avocado, sliced
- ½ lime, juiced
- 1 tsp ground cumin
- 2 tsp. chipotle paste

DIRECTIONS

1. Set aside the tomatoes, 1/4 onion, lime juice, and 1 tbsp oil. Fry the remaining onion in the remaining 2 tablespoons of oil until it softens. Fry for 1 minute, then add the garlic, cumin, and chipotle and stir until fragrant. Add the beans and a splash of water and simmer, occasionally stirring, until warm. Cook for 1 minute, starting in the majority of the tomato mixture, season well, and add the majority of the coriander.
2. Toast the bread and drizzle with 1 tbsp of the remaining oil. Arrange a piece on each plate and cover it with beans. To serve, arrange some avocado slices on top and garnish with the leftover tomato mixture and coriander leaves.

Sunshine smoothie

Preparation Time: 5 min

Serving: 3

28

INGREDIENTS

- 500ml carrot juice, chilled
- piece ginger, peeled
- 20g cashew nuts
- 1 lime juice
- 200g pineapple
- 2 bananas, broken into chunks

DIRECTIONS

1. Blend everything until it's smooth. Drink right away, or put some in a bottle to drink on the go. It will stay in the fridge for a day.

Vegan Smoothie

Preparation Time: 5 min

Serving: 2

INGREDIENTS

- 100ml cherry juice
- 3 tbsp. firm silken tofu
- 75g frozen cherry
- 2 tbsp. porridge oat
- 200ml unsweetened soya milk
- 1 cherry soya yogurt

DIRECTIONS

1. It doesn't matter if you measure everything exactly or use a tall glass and your empty yogurt pot for speed. They don't have to be exact. Blitz them until they're smooth. Then, pour into a tall glass (you'll have enough for a top-up) or two small glasses.

Smoky Cauliflower

Preparation Time: 30 min

Serving: 8

32

INGREDIENTS

- 2 tbsp. olive oil
- 1 tsp. smoked paprika
- 2 tbsp. Minced fresh parsley
- ¾ tsp. salt
- 1 head cauliflower, broken into florets
- 2 garlic cloves, minced

DIRECTIONS

1. Set the cauliflower in a big bowl and mix. Mix the oil, paprika, and salt. Cauliflower should be drenched in the sauce. Toss it around to coat. In a 15x10x1-inch baking pan, move the food. Bake at 450° for 10 minutes with the door open.
2. It's time for garlic to be added to the mix. Bake for another 10-15 minutes, stirring now and then until the cauliflower is soft and lightly browned. Sprinkle some parsley on it.

Grilled Lime-Balsamic Sweet Potatoes

Preparation Time: 25 min

Serving: 8

INGREDIENTS

- 2 tbsp. olive oil
- 1 tsp. salt
- ¼ cup packed brown sugar
- ¼ cup lime juice
- 3 tbsp. white or regular balsamic glaze
- 5 medium sweet potatoes
- ¼ tsp. pepper
- ¼ cup chopped fresh cilantro

DIRECTIONS

1. Peel each sweet potato and cut it in half lengthwise into eight wedges. Put them in a big bowl and mix them. Toss the food with oil, salt, and pepper.
2. Potatoes should be cooked in batches on a greased grill rack, covered, over medium heat for 8 to 10 minutes or until they are soft. Turn the potatoes every few minutes.
3. Large bowl: Add potatoes and toss to coat.

Vegan granola

Preparation Time: 30 min

Serving: 13

INGREDIENTS

- 150g coconut oil, melted
- 400g jumbo oats
- 2 tsp. cinnamon
- 250g pack mixed nuts, chopped
- 100ml maple syrup
- 150g dried apple, chopped

DIRECTIONS

1. Heat oven to 180C/160C fan/gas 4. Line 2 large-size baking trays with baking parchment. Mix all the ingredients except the maple syrup. Spread the granola out on the trays and drizzle over the maple syrup.
2. Bake in the oven for 20 mins, stirring the granola well halfway through so that it cooks evenly. Leave to cool before storing in a Kilner jar or airtight container. Best eaten within 1 month.

Vegan tomato & mushroom pancakes

Preparation Time: 38 min

Serving: 2

INGREDIENTS

- 400ml soya milk
- Vegetable oil for frying
- 140g white self-raising flour
- 1 tsp. soya flour

For the topping

- 2 tbsp. vegetable oil
- 2 tbsp. soya cream or soya milk
- Handful pine nuts
- Snipped chives to serve
- 250g button mushrooms
- 250g cherry tomatoes, halved

DIRECTIONS

1. In a blender, combine the flours and a pinch of salt. Blend in the soya milk until a smooth batter forms.
2. In a medium non-stick frying pan, heat a small amount of oil until very hot. Cook over medium heat, pour about 3 tbsp of the batter into the pa until bubbles develop on the surface of the pancake. Using a palette knife, flip the pancake over and cook on the other side until it is browned and crispy. Continue with the remaining batter, keeping the cooked pancakes warm between batches. You will make approximately 8.
3. Heat the oil in a frying pan for the topping. Simmer until the mushrooms are soft, add the tomatoes and cook for a few minutes longer. Add the soya cream or milk and pine nuts and simmer, stirring slowly, until mixed. Distribute the pancakes evenly between two dishes and top with the tomatoes and mushrooms. Sprinkle with chives.

Summer Porridge

Preparation Time: 20 min

Serving: 2

40

INGREDIENTS

- 1 kiwi fruit, cut into slices
- 200g blueberries
- ½ tbsp. maple syrup
- 50g pomegranate seeds
- 2 tsp. mixed seeds
- 300ml almond milk
- 2 tbsp. chia seeds
- 100g jumbo oats

DIRECTIONS

1. A blender is the best way to make purple milk. Put the milk, blueberries, and maple syrup in and blend until the milk turns purple. Pour blueberry milk into a bowl with the chia seeds and oats in it. Stir it very well. If you let the oatmeal and chia seeds soak, stir them now and then for about 5 minutes until the liquid has absorbed in, thickening them and making them grow bigger.
2. Stir it again, then divide it into two bowls. Arrange the fruit on top, then add the mixed seeds to the fridge for a day. Add the toppings right before you serve them.

Raspberry ripple chia pudding

Preparation Time: 18 min

Serving: 2

INGREDIENTS

- 50g white chia seeds
- 1 nectarine or peach, cut into slices
- 2 tbsp. goji berries
- 200ml coconut drinking milk

For the raspberry purée

- 2 tsp. maple syrup
- 100g raspberries
- 1 tsp. lemon juice

DIRECTIONS

1. In two bowls, mix the chia seeds and coconut milk. For about 5 minutes, stir the seeds now and then to make them swell and thicken when mixed with water. Then let them soak.
2. As long as you're doing that, mix up the purée ingredients. You can use a small-size mixer or a hand blender for this. Then put a spoonful in each bowl, place the nectarine peach slices on top, add the goji berries on top of that in the fridge for a day. Add the toppings right before you serve them.

Cardamom & peach quinoa porridge

Preparation Time: 23 min

Serving: 2

INGREDIENTS

- 75g quinoa
- 250ml unsweetened almond milk
- 2 ripe peaches, cut into slices
- 1 tsp maple syrup
- 25g porridge oats
- 4 cardamom pods

DIRECTIONS

1. Put the quinoa, oats, and cardamom pods in a small saucepan with 250ml water and 100ml almond milk. Set to a boil, then simmer gently for 15 mins, stirring occasionally.
2. Pour in the remaining almond milk and cook for 5 mins more until creamy.
3. Remove the cardamom pods, spoon into bowls or jars, and top with the peaches and maple syrup.

Vegan Lemon Poppy Scones

Preparation Time: 27 min

Serving: 12

INGREDIENTS

- 4 tsp. baking powder
- ½ tsp. salt
- 2 cups all-purpose flour
- 1 lemon, zested and juiced
- 2 tbsp. poppy seeds
- ½ cup soy milk
- ½ cup water
- ¾ cup white sugar
- ¾ cup vegan margarine

DIRECTIONS

1. Preheat oven range to 400 degrees Fahrenheit (200 degrees C). Grease a baking sheet with cooking spray.
2. Mix the baking powder, flour, sugar, and salt in a large mixing basin. Reduce the margarine until the mixture resembles huge grains of sand. I prefer to rub the margarine into the flour with my hands. Poppy seeds, lemon zest, and lemon juice should all be stirred. Mix the soy milk and water in a small bowl and gradually add to the dry ingredients, constantly stirring, until the batter is moistened but thick like biscuit dough. You may not require the entire amount of liquid.
3. Spoon 1/4 cup-sized dollops of batter about 3 inches apart onto the buttered baking sheet.
4. Bake for 15 minutes, or till golden, in a preheated oven.

Vegan Pancakes

Preparation Time: 15 min

Serving: 3

48

INGREDIENTS

- 1 tbsp. oil
- 1 ¼ cups all-purpose flour
- 1 ¼ cups water
- 2 tbsp. White sugar
- ½ tsp. salt
- 2 tsp. baking powder

DIRECTIONS

1. Mix the baking powder, flour, sugar, and salt in a large mixing basin.
2. In a small-size bowl, whisk together the water and oil. Make a well in the center of the dry ingredients and pour in the wet. Stir only until thoroughly combined; the mixture will be lumpy.
3. Over medium-high heat, heat a lightly greased skillet. Cook till bubbles form and the sides are dry, dropping batter by large spoonfuls onto the griddle. Cook until the other side is browned. Rep with the remainder of the batter.

Avocado Toast (Vegan)

Preparation Time: 10 min

Serving: 4

INGREDIENTS

- 1 ½ tsp. Extra-virgin olive oil
- ½ tsp. onion powder
- 1 avocado, halved and pitted
- 2 tbsp. Chopped fresh parsley
- ½ tsp. Garlic powder
- ½ lemon, juiced
- ½ tsp. salt
- 4 slices whole-grain bread
- ½ tsp. ground black pepper

DIRECTIONS

1. To toast bread in a toaster or toaster oven, use a toaster or toaster oven.
2. Scoop the avocados into a bowl.
3. Combine parsley, olive oil, lemon juice, salt, pepper, onion powder, and garlic powder using a potato masher. Spread each piece of toast with an avocado mixture.

Mango Craze Juice Blend

Preparation Time: 6 min

Serving: 4

INGREDIENTS

- 1 ½ cups chopped peaches
- ¼ cup chopped and pitted nectarine
- ½ cup orange juice
- 3 cups diced mango
- ¼ cup chopped orange segments
- 2 cups ice

DIRECTIONS

1. Place mango, peaches, orange, nectarine, orange juice, and ice into a blender. Blend for 1 minute or until smooth.

Hash with Smashed Potatoes and Tofu

Preparation Time: 30 min

Serving: 4

54

INGREDIENTS

- 3 tbsp. olive oil, divided
- ½ red bell pepper, diced
- 1 pinch ground black pepper
- 1 cup chopped kale
- 1 cup chopped cabbage
- ½ vonion, sliced
- 4 oz. firm tofu, crumbled
- 1 tbsp. soy sauce
- Salt and ground black pepper to taste
- 1 lb. potatoes

DIRECTIONS

1. In a large-size pot, combine potatoes and salted water; bring to a boil. Reduce to a standard-low heat and simmer for approximately 10 minutes, or until soft. Drain thoroughly in a colander.
2. On a grill or in a pan, warm 1 1/2 tablespoons olive oil. Add potatoes and carefully smash each one with the back of a spatula to about 1/2-inch thickness. Sear the potatoes on both sides until crispy, about 3 minutes. Transfer to a large bowl and season with pepper.
3. Meanwhile, heat the prevailing 1 1/2 teaspoons olive oil in a saute pan over medium-high heat. Sauté the kale, cabbage, onion, and bell pepper for around 3 minutes. Dust the tofu crumbles on top of the vegetables. Add soy sauce and boil until all liquid has evaporated, 3 to 5 minutes. Flavor with salt and pepper and serve alongside the mashed potatoes. Combine all ingredients and serve.

Oats with Chia Seeds and Fruit

Preparation Time: 12 min

Serving: 2

INGREDIENTS

- ¾ cup water
- 4 tbsp. chia seeds
- ½ tsp. ground cinnamon
- 1 ⅓ cups almond milk
- ¼ cup fresh blackberries
- 1 nectarine, peeled and diced
- 2 ripe bananas, mashed
- 1 ¼ cups rolled oats
- ¼ cup fresh blueberries

DIRECTIONS

1. In a pot or airtight container, combine almond milk, bananas, oats, water, chia seeds, and cinnamon; stir well. Refrigerate for 8 hours to overnight.
2. Cook the oat mixture in a saucepan over low heat for approximately 5 minutes. Distribute across two bowls and garnish with blueberries, blackberries, and nectarine.

Air Fryer Seasoned Breakfast Potatoes

Preparation Time: 35 min

Serving: 4

- 1 tbsp. Olive oil
- ½ tsp. Onion powder
- ½ tsp. paprika
- 1 lb. russet potatoes, peeled and cut into cubes
- 1 tsp. Salt
- ⅛ tsp. ground black pepper

DIRECTIONS

1. Place sliced potatoes in a bowl, cover them with cold water, and let them sit for about 30 minutes.
2. Heat it to 400 degrees F. (200 degrees C) when using an air fryer.
3. To dry the potatoes, use a paper towel. When you add olive oil and salt and onion powder and paprika and pepper, you'll get a good taste. Stir until everything is mixed together.
4. Take out your air fryer's basket and put the potatoes in it. Cook for 22 minutes, shaking the basket once during that time.

Eggless Crepes

Preparation Time: 25 min

Serving: 4

INGREDIENTS

- 1 tbsp. vegetable oil
- 1 cup all-purpose flour
- 1 tbsp. White sugar
- ¼ tsp. salt
- ½ cup skim milk
- ⅔ cup water
- ¼ cup butter, melted
- 2 tbsp. vanilla extract

DIRECTIONS

1. Whisk together milk, water, melted butter, and vanilla extract in a standard bowl. Mix sugar, flour, and salt thoroughly in a small bowl. Combine flour mixture and milk mixture in a separate bowl until the batter is smooth. Refrigerate for 2 hours, covered.
2. Preheat a medium skillet over medium-high heat. Coat pan lightly with vegetable oil and add roughly 2 tablespoons of crepe batter. Swirl pan to distribute the batter thinly. Cook until the sides are crispy and golden, then flip and cook until gently browned on the other side. Rep with the remainder of the batter.

Chocolate Coconut Overnight Oats

Preparation Time: 7 min

Serving: 1

INGREDIENTS

- 1 tbsp. chia seeds
- 1 tbsp. packed shredded sweetened coconut
- 1 cup chocolate-flavored almond milk
- 1 tbsp. maple syrup
- 1 tbsp. unsweetened cocoa powder
- 1 splash vanilla extract
- ¾ cup old-fashioned rolled oats

DIRECTIONS

1. Mix almond milk, oats, chia seeds, coconut, maple syrup, cocoa powder, and vanilla extract in a 12-ounce mason jar. Cover and refrigerate, 8 hours to overnight. Stir and serve cold.

Vegan Chocolate Banana Oatmeal

Preparation Time: 15 min

Serving: 1

INGREDIENTS

- ¾ cup cashew milk
- 1 tsp. unsweetened cocoa powder
- 1 pinch salt
- 2 tsp. maple syrup
- 1 tbsp. vegan dark chocolate chips
- ½ banana, sliced
- ¼ cup quick-cooking oats
- 1 pinch ground cinnamon

DIRECTIONS

1. Bring cashew milk to a boil in a saucepan over medium-high heat.
2. Reduce heat to low heat and add oats.
3. Combine cocoa powder, salt, and cinnamon in a large mixing bowl until well blended.
4. Use the maple syrup to sweeten. 5 minutes at low heat. Stir in chocolate chunks and continue cooking for an additional 1 to 2 minutes, or until the oatmeal reaches the desired consistency.
5. In a bowl, combine oats and bananas.

Quinoa Porridge

Preparation Time: 34 min

Serving: 3

INGREDIENTS

- ½ cup water
- 2 tbsp. Brown sugar
- ½ cup quinoa
- ¼ tsp. ground cinnamon
- 1 pinch salt
- 1 ½ cups almond milk
- 1 tsp. vanilla extract, Optional

DIRECTIONS

1. Over standard heat, melt the butter and add the quinoa to a skillet. Season with cinnamon and simmer for approximately 3 minutes, stirring often. Combine the almond milk, water, and vanilla extract in a large mixing bowl. Stir in the brown sugar and salt. Bring to a boil and cook over low heat for approximately 25 minutes, or until the porridge is thick and the grains are soft. If necessary, add additional water if the liquid has evaporated before the dish is finished cooking. Stir frequently, particularly near the end, to prevent scorching.

Vegan Crepes

Preparation Time: 26 min

Serving: 4

INGREDIENTS

- ¼ cup melted soy margarine
- ½ cup soy milk
- 1 cup unbleached all-purpose flour
- ¼ tsp. salt
- ½ cup water
- 1 tbsp. turbinado sugar
- 2 tbsp. maple syrup

DIRECTIONS

1. Blend the soy milk, water, 1/4 cup margarine, sugar, syrup, flour, and salt in a large mixing bowl. Wrap and Set aside the mixture for 2 hours.
2. Lightly grease a 5 to 6-inch skillet with some soy margarine. Heat the skillet until hot. Pour approximately 3 tablespoons batter into the skillet. Swirl to make the batter cover the skillet's bottom. Cook until golden, flip, and cook on the opposite side.

Mangu

Preparation Time: 40 min

Serving: 6

INGREDIENTS

- ¼ cup olive oil
- 3 green plantains
- 1 ½ tbsp. salt
- 1 cup sliced Anaheim peppers
- 1-quart water
- 1 cup sliced white onion

DIRECTIONS

1. In a saucepan, combine the plantains and water. Set to a boil, then reduce to low heat and cook for 20 minutes, or until the plantains are soft but somewhat hard. Drain the liquid, reserving 1 cup. Plantains and peels are excellent.
2. Heat the olive oil in a skillet over medium heat and sauté the onion until soft.
3. Mash the plantains in a basin with the saved liquid and salt.
4. Transfer to a food processor and purée with the peppers. Serve the pureed plantain mixture with onions on top.

Chickpea Mint Tabbouleh

Preparation Time: 30 min

Serving: 4

72

INGREDIENTS

- ¼ cup olive oil
- 1 cup peas, thawed
- 15 oz. chickpeas, rinsed and drained
- ½ cup minced fresh parsley
- 2 tbsp. julienned soft sun-dried tomatoes
- 2 tbsp. lemon juice
- ½ tsp. salt
- 1 cup bulgur
- 2 cups water
- ¼ cup minced fresh mint
- ¼ tsp. pepper

DIRECTIONS

1. Set bulgur and water to a boil in a big pot. Reduce to low heat and cover for 10 minutes. Stir in fresh or thawed peas; simmer, covered, for about 5 minutes, or until bulgur and peas are soft.
2. Transfer the mixture to a large bowl. Add the other ingredients and stir well. Serve warm or chilled.

Dijon Veggies with Couscous

Preparation Time: 42 min

Serving: 6

INGREDIENTS

- 2 tbsp. olive oil
- ¼ cup dry red wine or reduced-sodium chicken broth
- 3 tbsp. Dijon mustard
- ¼ tsp. pepper
- 2 garlic cloves, minced
- 1/2 lb. fresh mushrooms, quartered
- 1 tsp. Prepared horseradish
- ½ tsp. salt
- 1 zucchini, halved lengthwise and cut into slices
- 1 sweet red pepper, cut into pieces
- 1 cup water
- 1 cup uncooked couscous

DIRECTIONS

1. Place an 18x12-inch piece of heavy-duty foil on a large baking sheet.
2. Combine the mushrooms, zucchini, and red pepper in a large bowl. Drizzle over the wine, mustard, oil, garlic, horseradish, salt, and pepper mixture. Coat well; transfer to prepared baking sheet. Add a second large piece of foil on top. Bring the foil pieces together along their edges and crimp to secure, making a huge packet.
3. Bake 20-25 minutes at 350° or until vegetables are soft. Carefully open the foil to let steam escape.
4. Meanwhile, bring water to a boil in a small saucepan. Incorporate couscous. Take the pan from the heat; cover; set it aside for 5-10 minutes, or until the water has been absorbed. With a fork, fluff. Toss couscous and vegetables together in a large serving bowl.
5. Freeze option: Freeze couscous mixture in a freezer container once cooled. To use, defrost partially overnight in the refrigerator. Cover and microwave on high until thoroughly heated in a microwave-safe dish, adding 2-3 tablespoons of water to moisten.

Sauteed Squash with Tomatoes & Onions

Preparation Time: 20 min

Serving: 8

- 2 tbsp. olive oil
- 2 large tomatoes, chopped
- 1 medium onion, chopped
- 1 tsp. Salt
- ¼ tsp. pepper
- 4 medium zucchini, chopped

DIRECTIONS

1. In a standard-size skillet, heat the oil over standard-high heat. Add onion; cook and stir until tender, 2-4 minutes. Add zucchini; cook and stir for 3 minutes.
2. Stir in tomatoes, salt, and pepper; cook and stir until squash is tender, 4-6 minutes longer. Serve with a slotted spoon.

Green Salad with Berries

Preparation Time: 15 min

Serving: 4

INGREDIENTS

- 1 cup torn romaine
- ½ red onion, thinly sliced
- ½ cup chopped walnuts
- 2 green onions, chopped
- 1 cup fresh baby spinach
- 1 cup sliced fresh strawberries
- ½ cup sliced celery
- 1 cup fresh raspberries
- ¼ cup raspberry vinaigrette

DIRECTIONS

1. In a large bowl, combine the first 7 ingredients. To serve, drizzle with vinaigrette and toss to combine. Top with raspberries.

Basil & Heirloom Tomato Toss

Preparation Time: 15 min

Serving: 4

INGREDIENTS

- ¼ cup olive oil
- ¾ tsp. Salt
- ¼ tsp. Ground mustard
- ¼ tsp. pepper
- 3 tbsp. red wine vinegar
- 2 tsp. sugar
- 1 garlic clove, minced
- 1 sweet yellow pepper, cut into pieces
- ½ small red onion, sliced
- 2 heirloom tomatoes, cut into pieces
- 1 tbsp. chopped fresh basil

DIRECTIONS

1. In a large-size bowl, whisk the first seven elements until blended. Add remaining ingredients; toss gently to combine.

Black Bean & Sweet Potato Rice Bowls

Preparation Time: 33 min

Serving: 4

INGREDIENTS

- 1-1/2 cups water
- 3 tbsp. olive oil, divided
- 4 cups chopped fresh kale
- 15 oz. black beans, rinsed and drained
- 2 tbsp. Sweet chili sauce
- ¾ cup uncooked long-grain rice
- ¼ tsp. garlic salt
- 1 sweet potato, peeled and diced
- 1 red onion, chopped
- Lime wedges and additional sweet chili sauce, optional

DIRECTIONS

1. In a large saucepan, combine rice, garlic salt, and water; bring to a boil. Decrease to low heat and cover; cook for 20 minutes, or until water is absorbed and soft rice. Take off the heat and set aside for 5 minutes.
2. Meanwhile, heat 2 tablespoons of oil and sauté sweet potato over medium-high heat for 8 minutes. Cook and stir until the potato is cooked about 4-6 minutes. Cook and stir kale until tender, about 3-5 minutes. Add beans and heat thoroughly.
3. 2 tablespoons chili sauce and remaining oil, gently stirred into rice; add to potato mixture. Serve with lime wedges and extra chili sauce, if preferred.

Simple Vegetarian Slow-Cooked Beans

Preparation Time: 4hr 16 min

Serving:

INGREDIENTS

- ¾ tsp. salt
- 6 garlic cloves, minced
- 2 tsp. ground cumin
- 1/8 tsp. chili powder
- 62 oz. great northern beans, rinsed and drained
- 4 carrots, chopped
- 1 cup vegetable stock
- 1/3 cup minced fresh parsley
- 1 cup oil-packed sun-dried tomatoes, chopped
- 4 cups fresh baby spinach, chopped
- 1/3 cup minced fresh cilantro

DIRECTIONS

1. Combine the first seven elements in a 3-quart slow cooker. Cook on low for 4-5 hours, covered, or until carrots are soft, adding spinach and tomatoes during the final 10 minutes of cooking. Add the cilantro and parsley at this point.

Satisfying Tomato Soup

Preparation Time: 33 min

Serving: 4

86

INGREDIENTS

- 30 oz. diced tomatoes, undrained
- 1-1/2 cups water
- ¼ tsp. ground pepper
- 2 tsp. Brown sugar
- ½ tsp. Salt
- ½ tsp. Dried basil
- ¼ tsp. dried oregano
- 2 tsp. canola oil
- ¼ cup finely chopped onion
- ¼ cup finely chopped celery
- Minced fresh basil, optional

DIRECTIONS

1. In a large-size saucepan, heat the oil over standard-high heat. Add onion and celery; cook and stir until tender, 2-4 minutes. Add remaining ingredients, except for optional fresh basil. Bring to a boil. Reduce heat; simmer, uncovered, 10 minutes to allow flavors to blend.
2. Puree soup using an immersion blender. Or excellent soup slightly and puree in batches in a blender; return to pan and heat through. If desired, top with fresh minced basil.
3. Freeze option: Freeze cooled soup in freezer containers. To use, partially thaw in refrigerator overnight. Heat through in a saucepan, stirring occasionally; add water if necessary.

Spinach Rice

Preparation Time: 20 min

Serving: 2

INGREDIENTS

- 2 tbsp. olive oil
- ¾ cup water
- 1 tbsp. dried parsley flakes
- 1/8 tsp. pepper
- ½ cup uncooked instant rice
- 2 cups fresh baby spinach
- ½ cup chopped onion
- ¼-1/2 tsp. salt

DIRECTIONS

1. Heat oil over medium-high heat; saute onion until tender. Stir in water, parsley, salt, and pepper; bring to a boil. Stir in rice; top with spinach.
2. Cover; remove from heat. Let stand until rice is tender, 7-10 minutes. Stir to combine.

Moroccan Cauliflower and Almond Soup

Preparation Time: 6 hr 22 min

Serving: 8

INGREDIENTS

- ¾ cup sliced almonds, toasted and divided
- ½ cup + 2 tbsp. minced fresh cilantro, divided
- 1 head cauliflower, broken into florets
- 6 cups vegetable stock
- 2 tbsp. Olive oil
- ½ tsp. ground coriander
- 1-3 tsp. hot pepper sauce
- 1-1/4 tsp. Salt
- ½ tsp. Pepper
- ½ tsp. Ground cinnamon
- ½ tsp. ground cumin
- Additional harissa chili paste, optional

DIRECTIONS

1. Combine cauliflower, vegetable stock, 1/2 cup almonds, 1/2 cup cilantro, and the remaining 7 ingredients in a 5- or 6-quart slow cooker. Cook, wrapped, on low heat for 6 hours, or until cauliflower is soft.
2. Using an immersion blender, puree the soup. Alternatively, let the soup cool slightly before pureeing in batches in a blender; return to slow cooker and heat through. If preferred, serve with the remaining 1/4 cup almonds, 2 tbsp cilantro, and extra harissa.

Black Bean & Corn Quinoa

Preparation Time: 33 min

Serving: 4

INGREDIENTS

- 2 tbsp. canola oil
- 1 celery rib, finely chopped
- 2 tsp. Chili powder
- ¼ tsp. salt
- 1 cup quinoa, rinsed
- 15 oz. black beans, rinsed and drained
- 1/3 cup + 2 tbsp. minced fresh cilantro, divided
- 1 onion, chopped
- 1 medium sweet red pepper, chopped
- ¼ tsp. pepper
- 2 cups vegetable stock
- 1 cup frozen corn

DIRECTIONS

1. In a standard-size skillet, heat the oil over standard-high heat. Add onion, red pepper, celery, and seasonings; cook and stir 5-7 minutes or until vegetables are tender.
2. Stir in stock and corn; bring to a boil. Stir in quinoa. Reduce heat; simmer, covered, 12-15 minutes or until liquid is absorbed.
3. Add beans and 1/3 cup cilantro; heat through, stirring occasionally. Sprinkle with remaining cilantro.

Heirloom Tomato Salad

Preparation Time: 22 min

Serving: 6

- ½ tsp. maple syrup
- Pinch of sea salt
- ½ cup whole rolled oats
- ½ cup almona 2 cups cut-up heirloom tomatoes
- 2 cups fresh baby spinach
- ½ cup sliced red onion
- 1 cup multicolored cherry tomatoes, halved

Dressing:

- ¼ tsp. Dried thyme
- ¼ tsp. pepper
- 2 tbsp. white balsamic vinegar
- 3 tbsp. Olive oil
- ¼ tsp. dried rosemary, crushed
- 1 garlic clove, minced
- ½ tsp. Salt
- ¼ tsp. Dried basil
- ¼ tsp. dried oregano
- 1/8 tsp. rubbed sage
- d milk
- Desired toppings from above

DIRECTIONS

1. In a large-size pot, combine tomatoes, spinach, and onion. Combine dressing elements in a small pot; toss with salad. Refrigerate for 2 hours, covered. With a slotted spoon, serve.

Curried Lentil Soup

Preparation Time: 8 hr 16 min

Serving: 10

INGREDIENTS

- 4 cups water
- 28 oz. crushed tomatoes
- 3 potatoes, peeled and diced
- 4 tsp curry powder
- 2 bay leaves
- 2 garlic cloves, minced
- 3 carrots, sliced
- 1 cup dried lentils, rinsed
- 1 large onion, chopped
- 1 celery rib, chopped
- 1-1/4 tsp. salt

DIRECTIONS

1. In a 4- or 5-qt slow cooker, combine the first 10 ingredients. Wrap and cook on low for 8 hours or until vegetables and lentils are tender. Stir in salt. Discard bay leaves.

Arborio Rice and White Bean Soup

Preparation Time: 33 min

Serving: 4

INGREDIENTS

- ¼ tsp. dried oregano
- 16 oz. frozen broccoli-cauliflower blend
- ¾ cup uncooked arborio rice
- 32 oz. Vegetable broth
- ¾ tsp. dried basil
- 15 oz. cannellini beans, rinsed and drained
- 1 tbsp. olive oil
- 3 garlic cloves, minced
- ½ tsp. dried thyme
- 2 cups fresh baby spinach
- Lemon wedges, optional

DIRECTIONS

1. Sauté garlic in oil over standard heat for 1 minute. Cook and stir for 2 minutes. Bring to a boil, stirring in broth and herbs. Reduce to low heat and cook, covered, for approximately 10 minutes, or until rice is al dente.
2. Cook, covered, over medium heat, until cooked through and rice is soft, about 8-10 minutes, stirring occasionally. Add spinach and stir until wilted. Serve with lemon slices, if desired.

Vegetable Barley Saute

Preparation Time: 33 min

Serving: 4

INGREDIENTS

- 1 tbsp. canola oil
- 3 tbsp. reduced-sodium soy sauce
- 2 tsp. cornstarch
- 2 carrots, thinly sliced
- 1 cup cut fresh green beans
- ½ cup quick-cooking barley
- 1/3 cup water
- 1 garlic clove, minced
- 2 green onions, sliced
- ½ cup unsalted cashews, optional

DIRECTIONS

1. Prepare barley according to the directions on the box. Combine water, soy sauce, and cornstarch in a small dish until smooth; leave aside.
2. Sauté garlic in oil for 15 seconds in a large skillet or wok. Stir-fry carrots and beans for 2 minutes.
3. Add onions and continue to stir-fry for an additional minute. Incorporate soy sauce mixture into skillet.
4. Set to a boil; cook and stir for approximately 1 minute, or until thickened. Add barley and bring to a boil. Stir in cashews if desired.

Tomato Avocado Sandwich

Preparation Time: 10 min

Serving: 1

INGREDIENTS

- 1 slice ciabatta bread
- 3 slices tomato
- 1 pinch ground black pepper
- ½ avocado - peeled, pitted, and mashed
- 1 tsp. garlic salt

DIRECTIONS

1. Mix mashed avocado and garlic salt in a bowl; spread onto ciabatta bread. Layer tomatoes over avocado and top with black pepper.

Vegan Double Chocolate Protein Fudge

Preparation Time: 50 min

Serving: 12

INGREDIENTS

- ½ Cup raw almonds
- ¼ Cup unsweetened almond milk
- 1 cup natural vegan chocolate
- 2 tbsp. natural almond butter
- ¼ cup raw cocoa powder
- ½ Cup pitted dates
- 2 tbsp. steel-cut oats
- ½ cup figs, dried

DIRECTIONS

1. Combine the protein powder, chocolate powder, dates, figs, almond butter, and almond milk in a food processor. You may need to process the mixture for 10-20 seconds, scrape the sides, and process again until the mixture is sticky and moist.
2. Process the almonds and oats again until combined with the fudge mixture but the remaining pieces.
3. You may need to modify the processing time as you go since it will likely vary between food processors, but the result should be a sticky fudge-like mixture with bits of nuts and oats.
4. Line a baking sheet with a parchment sheet (I used an 8X8 pan) and spoon the fudge mixture into the prepared pan.
5. Smooth the fudge in the pan with wet hands or a spatula soaked in water. Cover more parchment paper and smooth over the top, pressing down to ensure the fudge is packed in an equal layer in the pan.
6. Freeze the fudge for 1 hour. Once firm, take off the parchment paper from the pan and cut it into squares or bars on a cutting board.
7. Refrigerate or freeze!

Yogurt with Pomegranate and Olive Oil

Preparation Time: 6 min

Serving: 1

INGREDIENTS

- 1tsp. olive oil
- ½ cup plain peanut yogurt
- 1tsp. parsley, chopped
- ½ cup pomegranate seeds

DIRECTIONS

1. Grab a medium ceramics bowl, and add plain peanut yogurt.
2. Now spread over the top of yogurt chopped parsley and pomegranate seeds.
3. In the end, drizzle olive oil overtopping and serve.

Avocado Toast with Cottage Cheese & Tomatoes

Preparation Time: 8 min

Serving: 4

INGREDIENTS

- 1 ripe California avocado
- 8 slices hearty whole grain bread
- 1 tomato, sliced
- Salt and pepper to taste
- 2 cups vegan cottage cheese

DIRECTIONS

1. On a large cutting board, arrange bread pieces and top each one with 14 cups of cottage cheese—season with salt and pepper to taste.
2. Season with an additional sprinkle of salt and pepper. Place tomato slices avocado on top of cottage cheese.
3. Serve by cutting bread pieces in half.

No-Bake Apple Pie Protein Bars

Preparation Time: 18 min

Serving: 12

INGREDIENTS

- ½ Cup unsweetened applesauce
- 1 tbsp. coconut milk
- ¼ cup almond butter
- ½ cup maple syrup
- 1 cup coconut flour
- ½ cup almond flour
- 1 tsp. mixed spice
- 1 tsp. nutmeg
- ½ cup protein powder
- 2 tbsp. granulated sweetener
- 1 tbsp. cinnamon

DIRECTIONS

1. Prepare a big baking dish by lining it with oiled parchment paper and setting it aside.
2. Combine the flour, protein powder, granulated sugar, cinnamon, nutmeg, and mixed spice in a large mixing bowl and stir well.
3. Combine the nut butter and liquid sweetener in a microwave-safe bowl and heat until melted. Combine the wet and dry ingredients well. Combine the unsweetened applesauce and flour in a large mixing bowl until well combined—the mixture should be crumbly.
4. Add the coconut milk 1 spoonful at a time with a spoon until a thick, solid batter forms.
5. Transfer to a parchment-lined baking dish and firmly press. Refrigerate for at least 30 minutes before serving.

Ham and Cheese Baked Cups

Preparation Time: 45 min

Serving: 12

112

INGREDIENTS

- ¼ cup minced scallions
- 4 oz. shredded sharp peanut butter
- 6 slices of vegan bacon (any plant)
- ½ cup Applesauce
- ½ cup coconut milk
- Salt and pepper

DIRECTIONS

1. Preheat the cooking ring to 350 degrees, spray a muffin pan with cooking spray or use a silicone pan.
2. Whisk together applesauce and milk until light and fluffy in a large pot. To taste, stir in the Canadian bacon, scallions, and salt/pepper.
3. Split the Applesauce mixture evenly between 12 muffin pans (about 13 cups each) and top with strong cheddar cheese. Bake until eggs are set, 25-30 minutes. Let cool slightly to ensure eggs are set before removing from pan to serve.

Crispy Tofu with Black Pepper Sauce

Preparation Time: 30 min

Serving: 4

INGREDIENTS

- 2 tbsp. reduced-sodium soy sauce
- 1 tbsp. packed brown sugar
- 1 tbsp. rice vinegar
- 2 tbsp. chili garlic sauce
- 6 tbsp. canola oil, divided
- 4 green onions
- 8 oz. fresh sugar snap peas, trimmed and sliced
- 1 tsp. ground pepper
- 3 garlic cloves, minced
- 8 oz. extra-firm tofu, drained
- 3 tbsp. cornstarch
- 2 tsp. grated fresh ginger root

DIRECTIONS

1. Combine the first four elements in a mixing bowl. Mince the green onion whites; Slice the green bits lightly.
2. Tofu should be cut into 1/2-inch cubes and patted dry with paper towels. Toss tofu in cornstarch mixture. Heat 4 tablespoons oil in a large skillet over medium-high heat. Cook, stirring until tofu is crisp and golden brown, about 5-7 minutes. Remove from pan and pat dry with paper towels.
3. Heat the 1 tablespoon oil in the same pan over medium-high heat. Stir-fry peas for 2-3 minutes, or until crisp-tender. Take out of the pan.
4. Heat the remaining 1 tablespoon oil over medium-high heat in the same pan. Cook for 30 seconds before adding pepper. Stir-fry the garlic, ginger, and minced green onions for 30 to 45 seconds. Add soy sauce mixture and simmer, constantly stirring, until slightly thickened. Turn off the heat and mix in the tofu and peas. Garnish with thinly sliced green onions.

Couscous with Olives and Sun-Dried Tomato

Preparation Time: 50 min

Serving: 4

INGREDIENTS

- 5 tbsp. olive oil, divided
- ½ cup pine nuts
- 4 cloves garlic, minced
- ⅓ cup sun-dried tomatoes packed in oil, drained and chopped
- 1 shallot, minced
- 1 ¼ cups vegetable broth
- 1 cup vegetable broth
- 1 ¼ cups water
- 2 cups pearl couscous
- 1 pinch salt
- ¼ cup chopped fresh flat-leaf parsley
- 1 pinch ground black pepper
- ½ cup sliced black olives

DIRECTIONS

1. In a saucepan, bring 1 1/4 cup vegetable broth and water to a boil. Stir in couscous and season with salt and black pepper. Decrease to low heat and simmer for approximately 8 minutes, or until liquid is absorbed.
2. In a skillet over standard-high heat, heat 3 tablespoons olive oil; add pine nuts and cook, tossing regularly, until pine nuts smell toasted and are golden brown, about 1 minute. Take the pan off the heat.
3. In a saucepan, heat the prevailing 2 tbsp olive oil; sauté, stir garlic, and shallot until softened, about 2 minutes. Cook, frequently tossing, until black olives and sun-dried tomatoes are heated for about 2 to 3 minutes. Add 1 cup vegetable broth gradually and bring to a boil. Decrease to low heat and simmer for 8 to 10 minutes, or until the sauce has reduced.
4. Transfer couscous to a large serving dish, stir with sauce and serve with parsley and pine nuts on top.

Vegan Red Lentil Soup

Preparation Time: 55 min

Serving: 4

118

INGREDIENTS

- 14 oz. coconut milk
- 2 tbsp. tomato paste
- 1 tsp. curry powder
- 1 small onion, chopped
- 1 cup dry red lentils
- 1 tbsp. minced fresh ginger root
- 1 pinch ground nutmeg
- 1 cup butternut squash - peeled, seeded, and cubed
- 1 tbsp. peanut oil
- 1 clove garlic, chopped
- Salt and pepper to taste
- ⅓ cup chopped fresh cilantro
- 1 pinch fenugreek seeds
- 2 cups water
- 1 pinch cayenne pepper

DIRECTIONS

1. Cook the onion, ginger, garlic, and fenugreek in the oil over medium heat until the onion is soft.
2. In the pot, combine the lentils, squash, and cilantro. Combine the water, coconut milk, and tomato paste in a medium bowl. Curry powder, cayenne pepper, nutmeg, salt, and pepper to taste. Bring to a boil, reduce to low heat, and continue cooking for 30 minutes, or until lentils and squash are cooked.

Black Bean and Corn Salad

Preparation Time: 27 min

Serving: 6

INGREDIENTS

- 6 green onions, sliced
- ½ cup olive oil
- 1 clove garlic, minced
- ⅓ cup fresh lime juice
- 1 avocado - peeled, pitted, and diced
- 1 red bell pepper, chopped
- 2 tomatoes, chopped
- 1 tsp. salt
- ⅛ tsp. ground cayenne pepper
- 15 oz. black beans, rinsed and drained
- 1 ½ cups frozen corn kernels
- ½ cup chopped fresh cilantro, Optional

DIRECTIONS

1. Combine lime juice, olive oil, garlic, salt, and cayenne pepper in a small container. Cover with a cover and shake vigorously until all ingredients are thoroughly combined.
2. Combine beans, corn, avocado, bell pepper, tomatoes, green onions, and cilantro in a salad dish. Shake the lime dressing vigorously and drizzle it over the salad. Serve salad, stirring to cover vegetables and beans with sauce.

Easy Guacamole

Preparation Time: 40 min   **Serving: 16**

INGREDIENTS

- 1 ripe tomato, chopped
- 1 small onion, chopped
- 1 lime, juiced
- 2 avocados
- 1 clove garlic, minced
- Salt and pepper

DIRECTIONS

1. In a medium-sized serving basin, peel and mash avocados. Combine the onion, garlic, tomato, lime juice, salt, and pepper in a medium bowl. Season with the remainder of the lime juice and season with salt and pepper to taste. Refrigerate for a half hour to allow flavors to mingle.

Quinoa Tabbouleh

Preparation Time: 30 min

Serving: 4

INGREDIENTS

- ¼ cup olive oil
- ½ tsp. sea salt
- 2 carrots, grated
- 2 cups water
- 1 cup quinoa
- 1 pinch salt
- 2 bunches of green onions, diced
- 1 cup chopped fresh parsley
- ¼ cup lemon juice
- 3 tomatoes, diced
- 1 cucumber, diced

DIRECTIONS

1. In a saucepan, bring water to a boil. Add quinoa and a pinch of salt. Decrease the heat to low, cover, and simmer for 15 minutes. Allow to cool to room temperature; fluff with a fork.
2. Meanwhile, combine olive oil, sea salt, lemon juice, tomatoes, cucumber, green onions, carrots, and parsley in a large bowl. Stir in cooled quinoa.

Baked Tofu Bites

Preparation Time: 25 min

Serving: 4

INGREDIENTS

- 1 tbsp. Sesame seeds
- ¼ tsp. garlic powder
- 2 tbsp. maple syrup
- 2 tbsp. Ketchup
- ¼ tsp. ground black pepper
- 16 oz. extra firm tofu
- ¼ cup soy sauce
- 1 tbsp. vinegar
- 1 dash hot sauce
- 1 tsp. liquid smoke flavoring

DIRECTIONS

1. Preheat oven range to 375 degrees F (190 degrees C). Lightly spray a non-stick baking sheet with oil.
2. Slice tofu into 1/2-inch slices, and gently press the excess water out of tofu. Cut sliced tofu into 1/2-inch cubes.
3. Stir together the soy sauce, maple syrup, ketchup, vinegar, and hot sauce in a bowl. Stir in sesame seeds, garlic powder, black pepper, and liquid smoke. Gently stir tofu cubes into the sauce. Cover, and marinate for at least 5 minutes.
4. Place the tofu on the baking sheet in a single layer. Bake in a preheated oven for 15 minutes. Turn tofu, and bake until the tofu turns golden brown, about 15 minutes more.

Vegan Cupcakes

Preparation Time: 25 min

Serving: 18

INGREDIENTS

- ½ cup coconut oil warmed until liquid
- 2 cups all-purpose flour
- 1 cup white sugar
- 2 tsp. baking powder
- 1 ¼ tsp. vanilla extract
- 1 tbsp. apple cider vinegar
- 1 ½ cups almond milk
- ½ tsp. Baking soda
- ½ tsp. salt

DIRECTIONS

1. Preheat oven range to 350 degrees F (175 degrees C). Grease two 12 cup muffin pans or line with 18 paper baking cups.
2. Measure the apple cider vinegar into a 2 cup measuring cup. Fill with almond milk to make 1 1/2 cups. Let stand until curdled, about 5 minutes. Mix the baking soda, flour, sugar, baking powder, and salt in a large bowl. Whisk the almond milk mixture, coconut oil, and vanilla in a separate bowl. Pour the wet elements into the dry ingredients and stir just until blended. Pour the batter into the prepared muffin cups, distributing it evenly.
3. Bake in the preheated range until the tops spring back for 15 to 20 minutes when lightly pressed. Cool on a wire rack. Place cooled cupcakes on a serving plate. Frost as desired.

Vegan Bean Taco Filling

Preparation Time: 30 min

Serving: 8

130

INGREDIENTS

- 1 tbsp. olive oil
- 2 tbsp. yellow cornmeal
- 1 ½ tbsp. cumin
- 1 bell pepper, chopped
- 14.5 oz. black beans, rinsed, drained, and mashed
- 1 tsp. paprika
- 1 tsp. cayenne pepper
- 1 tsp. chili powder
- 1 cup salsa
- 1 onion, diced
- 2 cloves garlic, minced

DIRECTIONS

1. Heat olive oil in a standard skillet over medium heat. Stir in onion, garlic, and bell pepper; cook until tender. Stir in mashed beans. Add the cornmeal. Mix in cumin, paprika, cayenne, chili powder, and salsa. Cover, and cook for 5 minutes.

Vegan Mug Cake

Preparation Time: 8 min

Serving: 1

INGREDIENTS

- 3 tbsp. soy milk
- 2 tbsp. Unsweetened cocoa powder
- ¼ tsp. baking powder
- 1 tbsp. vegan chocolate chips
- 4 tbsp. all-purpose flour
- 3 tbsp. white sugar
- 4 tbsp. applesauce
- 1 tbsp. toasted flaked coconut, Optional

DIRECTIONS

1. Combine the flour, sugar, cocoa powder, and baking powder in a cup. In a bowl, combine applesauce and soy milk; add to flour mixture. Stir well until thoroughly blended. Combine chocolate chips and coconut in a large mixing bowl.
2. Microwave on the highest setting for approximately 3 minutes, or until the mug cake has set and risen well.

Easy Vegan Pasta with Kale and Chickpeas

Preparation Time: 25 min

Serving: 4

INGREDIENTS

- ¼ cup olive oil
- 16 oz. spaghetti
- 2 tbsp. nutritional yeast
- 15 oz. chickpeas
- Salt and ground black pepper
- 5 cloves garlic, minced
- 1 bunch kale, chopped

DIRECTIONS

1. Set a large-size pot of lightly salted water to a boil. Cook spaghetti in the boiling water, occasionally stirring, until tender yet firm to the bite, about 12 minutes. Drain, reserving about 1 cup of the cooking water.
2. Heat olive oil in a large-size skillet over standard heat and cook garlic until fragrant, about 1 minute. Add kale and cook, constantly stirring, until wilted, about 3 minutes.
3. Stir cooked spaghetti into the skillet. Add nutritional yeast. Add enough of the reserved cooking water to create a thick sauce. Stir well. Add chickpeas and heat until warmed, 2 to 4 minutes. Season with salt and pepper.

Ginger Veggie Stir-Fry

Preparation Time: 40 min

Serving: 6

INGREDIENTS

- ¼ cup vegetable oil, divided
- ¼ cup chopped onion
- ½ tbsp. salt
- 1 head broccoli, cut into florets
- ½ cup snow peas
- ¾ cup julienned carrots
- 1 tbsp. cornstarch
- 1 ½ cloves garlic, crushed
- 2 tsp. chopped fresh ginger root, divided
- ½ cup halved green beans
- 2 tbsp. soy sauce
- 2 ½ tbsp. water

DIRECTIONS

1. In a large bowl, blend cornstarch, garlic, 1 teaspoon ginger, and 2 tablespoons vegetable oil until cornstarch is dissolved. Mix in broccoli, snow peas, carrots, and green beans, tossing to coat lightly.
2. Heat remaining 2 tablespoons oil in a large-size skillet or wok over medium heat. Cook vegetables in oil for 2 minutes, constantly stirring to prevent burning. Stir in soy sauce and water. Mix in onion, salt, and the remaining 1 teaspoon ginger. Cook until vegetables are tender but still crisp.

White Bean Fennel Soup

Preparation Time: 55 min

Serving: 5

- 14-1/2 oz. diced tomatoes, undrained
- 1 tbsp. olive oil
- 5 cups reduced-sodium vegetable broth
- 1 large onion, chopped
- ¼ tsp pepper
- 1 bay leaf
- 3 cups shredded fresh spinach
- 1 small fennel bulb, thinly sliced
- 15 oz. cannellini beans, rinsed and drained
- 1 tsp. dried thyme

DIRECTIONS

1. Sauté onion and fennel in oil in a large pot until soft. Bring the broth, beans, tomatoes, thyme, pepper, and bay leaf to a boil. Decrease to low heat and cover; cook for 30 minutes or until the soft fennel.
2. Remove bay leaf. Cook for an additional 3-4 minutes, or until spinach is wilted.

Romaine & Orange Salad with Lime Dressing

Preparation Time: 16 min

Serving: 6

INGREDIENTS

- 2 tbsp. olive oil
- 1 small garlic clove, minced
- 1/8 tsp. salt
- 1 tbsp. Lime juice
- ¾ tsp. sugar
- 1/8 tsp. grated lime zest
- ½ cup sliced red onion
- 11 oz. mandarin oranges, drained
- 6 cups torn romaine

DIRECTIONS

1. In a small-size bowl, whisk the first six elements. Combine romaine and onion in a large bowl. Drizzle dressing over and toss to coat. Mandarin oranges on top Serve right away.

Barley Corn Salad

Preparation Time: 18 min

Serving: 6

INGREDIENTS

- ½ cup chopped green pepper
- 3 green onions, chopped
- 2 cups cooked medium pearl barley
- 2 cups frozen corn, thawed
- ½ cup chopped sweet red pepper
- 1 tbsp. minced fresh cilantro
- 2 tbsp. Canola oil
- ½ tsp. salt
- 1/8 tsp. pepper
- 2 tbsp. Lemon juice
- ½ tsp. dried thyme

DIRECTIONS

1. In a large-size bowl, combine the first 6 elements. Toss all of the ingredients in a mason jar with a tight-fitting lid until everything is well combined; then set aside. Drizzle over salad and toss to coat. Cover and refrigerate for at least 2 hours before serving.
2. Freeze option: Prepare salad without onions and cilantro. Transfer to freezer containers; freeze. To use, thaw completely in the refrigerator. Gently stir in onions, cilantro, and a little oil if necessary.

Garlic-Herb Pattypan Squash

Preparation Time: 26 min

Serving: 4

144

INGREDIENTS

- 1 tbsp. Olive oil
- ¼ tsp. pepper
- 1 tbsp. minced fresh parsley
- 2 garlic cloves, minced
- ½ tsp. salt
- 5 cups halved small pattypan squash
- ¼ tsp. Dried oregano
- ¼ tsp. dried thyme

DIRECTIONS

1. Preheat oven to 425 degrees Fahrenheit. Place the squash in a greased 15x10x1-inch baking dish. Pan for baking. Drizzle squash with oil, garlic, salt, oregano, thyme, and pepper. To coat, toss. Roast for 15-20 minutes, tossing periodically, or until tender. Parsley, if desired.

Rice Pilaf with Apples & Raisins

Preparation Time: 26 min

Serving: 4

INGREDIENTS

- 2 tbsp. olive oil
- 1-1/2 cups water
- ¼ cup chopped dried apples
- ¼ cup golden raisins
- 1 tsp. Salt
- ¼ tsp. Ground allspice
- ¼ tsp. Ground cinnamon
- ¼ tsp. dried thyme
- 1 onion, chopped
- 1 cup uncooked jasmine rice
- 1/8 tsp. cayenne pepper

DIRECTIONS

1. Heat oil over standard heat; saute onion until tender, 4-6 minutes. Put rice; cook and stir until golden browned 4-6 minutes.
2. Stir in remaining ingredients; bring to a boil. Reduce heat; simmer, covered until liquid is absorbed and rice is tender 15-20 minutes. Fluff with a fork.

Asparagus, Squash & Red Pepper Saute

Preparation Time: 30 min

Serving: 4

148

INGREDIENTS

- 4-1/2 tsp. olive oil
- 6 oz. Fresh asparagus, trimmed and cut into pieces
- ¼ cup white wine or vegetable broth
- ¼ tsp. salt
- 2 sweet red peppers, julienned
- 2 yellow summer squash, halved and cut into slices
- ¼ tsp. pepper

DIRECTIONS

1. In a large cast-iron or another heavy skillet, saute the peppers, squash, and asparagus in wine and oil until crisp-tender. Sprinkle with salt and pepper.

Curried Quinoa And Chickpeas

Preparation Time: 42 min

Serving: 4

INGREDIENTS

- 1-1/2 cups water
- 2 tomatoes, seeded and chopped
- 1 sweet red pepper, julienned
- 1 small red onion, chopped
- ½ cup raisins
- 1 tsp. curry powder
- ½ cup minced fresh cilantro
- ½ cup orange juice
- 15 oz. chickpeas, rinsed and drained
- 1 cup quinoa, rinsed

DIRECTIONS

1. Set water and orange juice to a boil in a big saucepan. Combine chickpeas, tomatoes, red pepper, quinoa, onion, raisins, and curry in a medium mixing bowl. Return to a specific location. Cover and cook for 15-20 minutes, or until all of the liquid has been absorbed. Reduce heat to low and cook for 20 minutes.
2. Take off the pan from the heat and fluff with a fork. Serve garnished with cilantro.

Gnocchi With Pesto Sauce

Preparation Time: 26 min

Serving: 4

INGREDIENTS

- ½ cup chopped sweet yellow pepper
- 2 tsp. olive oil
- ¼ cup prepared pesto
- 1 cup chopped tomatoes
- 16 oz. potato gnocchi
- 1 cup diced zucchini
- Toasted pine nuts, optional

DIRECTIONS

1. Cook gnocchi according to package directions; drain.
2. Meanwhile, heat oil over medium-high heat; saute zucchini and pepper until zucchini is tender.
3. Add pesto and gnocchi, stirring gently to coat. Stir in tomatoes. If desired, top with pine nuts.

Salsa Bean Burgers

Preparation Time: 25 min

Serving: 4

INGREDIENTS

- 2 tsp. canola oil
- ½ cup Applesauce
- 2 tbsp. minced fresh cilantro
- 4 whole-wheat hamburger buns, split
- 15 oz. black beans, rinsed and drained
- ¾ cup panko bread crumbs
- 1 cup salsa, divided
- 1 garlic clove, minced

DIRECTIONS

1. In a large bowl, mash the beans. Mix bread crumbs, 1/2 cup salsa, applesauce, cilantro, and garlic. Shape bean mixture into 4 patties; refrigerate for 30 minutes.
2. In a large-size skillet, heat the oil over medium heat. Cook burgers for 6 minutes per side or till a thermometer reads 160°. Serve on buns with remaining salsa.

Easy Singapore Noodles

Preparation Time: 30 min

Serving: 4

INGREDIENTS

- 1 tbsp. sunflower or vegetable oil
- 1 onion, sliced
- 1 tsp. caster sugar
- 1 tbsp. sesame oil
- 2½ tbsp. low-salt soy sauce
- 1 pepper, sliced
- 200g beansprouts
- 200g vermicelli rice noodles
- 1 tbsp. Mild curry powder
- ¼ tsp. turmeric
- 1 red chili, sliced, optional

DIRECTIONS

1. Bring the kettle to a boil and transfer the noodles to a wide pan or bowl. Add enough boiling water to cover the noodles, pressing them under the water to help them soften uniformly. Remove from heat and set aside for 5-10 minutes, or until the noodles are soft. Combine the curry powder, turmeric, sugar, sesame oil, soy sauce, and 1 tablespoon water in a pot.

2. Preheat the wok to high heat. Combine the sunflower oil, onion, and pepper in a medium bowl. Stir-fry for 4 minutes, or till softened and beginning to brown in spots. Drain the noodles and add the sauce mixture and beansprouts to the pan. Stir-fry for an additional 3-4 minutes, stirring everything in the sauce until everything is heated. Season with extra soy or sugar and scatter over the chills if desired.

Salt & Pepper Tofu

Preparation Time: 36 min

Serving: 4

158

INGREDIENTS

- Sesame oil for drizzling
- 2 red peppers, sliced
- 2 tbsp. vegetable oil
- A handful of coriander leaves picked
- ¼ broccoli head, cut into florets
- 396g pack firm tofu
- 2 tbsp. cornflour
- 1 tsp. black peppercorns, ground to a powder
- 100g beansprouts
- 2 tsp. low-salt soy sauce

DIRECTIONS

1. Drain the tofu and place it loosely wrapped in kitchen paper on a platter. Place a chopping board on top. If you're using a light chopping board, weigh it down with a couple of cans; otherwise, a heavier chopping board would suffice. Allow 10-20 minutes for the cloth to become damp from the surplus liquid. Pressing the tofu in this manner imparts a firmer firmness after being cooked.
2. Cut the tofu in half horizontally down the center as if it were a book. Each piece should be cut into four triangles, similar to a piece of toast, and then in half again to create 16 details in total. Combine the cornflour, ground pepper, and 1 teaspoon flaky sea salt on a dish. To coat each piece of tofu, gently turn it in the cornflour mixture.
3. In a wok, heat the 1 tbsp oil. For a few minutes, stir-fry the peppers and broccoli to soften slightly.
4. Combine the beansprouts and soy sauce in a medium bowl. Cook for another 1-2 minutes, checking to ensure the vegetables retain their crunch. Drizzle a small-size amount of sesame oil on top.
5. In a large non-stick frying pan, heat the remaining sunflower oil and cook the coated tofu for 5 minutes on each side, or until crisp. Serve garnished with coriander on top of the vegetables.

Beetroot & Red Onion Tarte Tatin

 Preparation Time: 1 hr 30 min

 Serving: 6

INGREDIENTS

- 3 tbsp. olive oil
- 1 orange, zested
- Peppery green salad, to serve
- 2 tbsp. rice wine vinegar
- 2 tbsp. soft brown sugar
- 2-star anise
- Flour, for rolling
- 400g beetroot, cut into wedges
- 1 red onion, cut into wedges
- 500g block puff pastry

DIRECTIONS

1. Preheat range to 200 degrees Celsius/180 degrees celsius fan/gas 6. Combine the beetroot and onion with 2 tbsp of the oil, vinegar, and sugar in a bowl. Season with star anise. In a large, ovenproof non-stick frying pan, heat the remaining oil and nestle in the vegetables, covering the entire surface of the pan. Wrap with foil and bake for 45 minutes.

2. Turn the pastry to a thickness of 0.5cm on a well-floured board and cut out a circle the same size as your frying pan. Remove the pan from the oven carefully, peel away the foil, and jiggle the beets and onion in the pan to form a compact layer. Return the pan to the range and bake for 35 minutes, or until the pastry has risen and is a deep golden brown.

3. Wrap a palette knife around the tart's edge, then place a plate on top, serving side down. To turn the pie out onto the plate, flip the pan over - take care not to burn yourself on the handle. Serve with a dusting of sea salt and orange zest on top and a peppery salad on the side.

Smoked Gouda Cheese Sauce

Preparation Time: 18 min

Serving: 2

INGREDIENTS

- 1 cup milk
- ½ cup Smoked Gouda, shredded
- ½ tsp. salt
- Smoked Gouda Cheese Sauce
- 2 tbsp. butter
- 2 tbsp. flour

DIRECTIONS

1. Melt the butter in a small-size saucepan over low heat to make the cheese sauce.
2. Stir in the flour until thoroughly combined and smooth.
3. Add the milk and whisk it into the butter and flour mixture. Bring the mixture to a boil over medium heat. Then turn down the heat. Decrease to low heat and cook for 2-3 minutes or thicken.
4. Turn off the heat and add the shredded cheese and salt to the pot. Stir constantly until the cheese is melted.

Vegan Tacos with Smoky Chipotle Portobellos

Preparation Time: 32 min

Serving: 2

INGREDIENTS

- 4 tortillas warmed
- 1 red bell pepper
- 2 extra-large portobello mushrooms
- 2 tbsp. canned Chipotle in Adobo sauce
- 1 chopped garlic clove
- 1 can refry black beans warmed
- ½ small red onion
- ½ tsp. Cumin
- ½ tsp. coriander
- Salt to taste
- 1 tbsp. oil

DIRECTIONS

1. Preheat oven to 425 degrees Fahrenheit.
2. Cut the portobellos into 12 inch thick wedges, and cut the bell peppers into 12 broad strips. Cut onion into 12 inch thick rings or half-moons if using.
3. Arrange everything on a parchment-lined sheet pan and whisk the marinade ingredients in a small bowl.
4. Brush the marinade liberally on both sides of the mushrooms, then lightly on the remaining red bell pepper and onion. Season portobellos liberally with salt. Roast for 20 minutes or until portobellos is tender when pierced with a fork. Heat the beans and prepare any other garnishes while this roasts. Both pickled onions and vegan cilantro crema take approximately ten minutes to prepare. Alternatively, Use the avocado slices.
5. When ready to serve, reheat the tortillas (on a gas stove or in a toaster oven) and cover liberally with the refried black beans. Distribute the chipotle portobellos and peppers (and, if using, the onions) among the tortillas. Drizzle the cilantro Crema, Poblano Salsa, avocado, fresh cilantro, and optional pickled onions on top.

Vegan Tofu Scramble

Preparation Time: 33 min

Serving: 1

INGREDIENTS

- ¼ cup red pepper (chopped)
- 175 grams tofu (medium-firm or firm)
- ½ tsp. Chili powder
- ½ tsp. dry mustard
- 1 tbsp. nutritional yeast
- ¼ cup green pepper (chopped)
- ½ cup mushrooms (chopped)
- ¼ tsp. Garlic powder
- ¼ tsp. turmeric
- 2 tbsp. almond or oat milk
- 1 tbsp. scallions (chopped)
- ⅛ tsp. ground black pepper
- Pinch of salt (to taste, optional)

DIRECTIONS

1. In a pan, combine chopped peppers and mushrooms. On a medium heat setting, cook for 5-10 minutes. Stir occasionally and, if necessary, add a splash of water to prevent sticking.
2. While the vegetables simmer, drain, and mash the tofu in a bowl. I simply pinch it between my palms. Additionally, you might use a fork or masher.
3. Combine the other ingredients in the bowl with the tofu.
4. After 5-10 minutes, add the tofu mixture to the pan and continue heating for an additional 5 minutes. Combine everything in the pan while it is cooking. If sticking occurs, a small amount more plant milk or put the water.
5. Take off the skillet from the heat after the tofu scramble is ready. Alternatively, garnish with avocado and more onions.

Green Salad with Edamame & Beets

Preparation Time: 18 min

Serving: 1

168

INGREDIENTS

- Freshly ground pepper to taste
- 2 cups mixed salad greens
- 2 tsp. extra-virgin olive oil
- ½ raw beet, peeled and shredded
- 1 tbsp. + 1 ½ tsp. red-wine vinegar
- 1 tbsp. chopped fresh cilantro
- 1 cup shelled edamame, thawed

DIRECTIONS

1. Prepare a big platter by arranging the greens, edamame, and beet. Whisk together the vinegar, cilantro, oil, salt, and pepper in a small-size bowl. Spray the dressing over the salad and serve.

Colorful Roasted Sheet-Pan Veggies

Preparation Time: 50 min

Serving: 4

INGREDIENTS

- 3 tbsp. extra-virgin olive oil, divided
- 4 cups broccoli florets
- 3 cups cubed butternut squash (1-inch)
- 1 tsp. Coarse kosher salt
- ¼ tsp. pepper
- 1 tbsp. best-quality balsamic vinegar
- 2 red bell peppers, cut into squares
- 1 red onion, cut into bite-size chunks
- 2 tsp. Italian seasoning

DIRECTIONS

1. Preheat the oven to 425 degrees Fahrenheit.
2. In a large mixing basin, combine squash and 1 tablespoon oil. Distribute evenly on a baking pan. 10 minutes roasting
3. Meanwhile, in a bowl with the remaining 2 tablespoons olive oil, stir broccoli, bell peppers, onion, Italian seasoning (or herbes de Provence), salt, and pepper until the veggies are uniformly coated.
4. Combine the squash with the remaining vegetables in the bowl. To blend, toss. Evenly divide the vegetables between two baking sheets. Roast for 17 to 20 minutes, stirring once or twice, or until the vegetables are tender and browned in spots. Drizzle vinegar over the entire surface.

Roasted Veggie & Tofu Brown Rice Bowl

 Preparation Time: 8 min

 Serving: 1

INGREDIENTS

- ½ cup cooked brown rice
- 1 cup roasted vegetables
- 1 cup roasted tofu
- 2 tbsp. sliced scallions
- 2 tbsp. chopped fresh cilantro
- 2 tbsp. Creamy Vegan Cashew Sauce

DIRECTIONS

1. Combine the rice, vegetables, and tofu in a large mixing bowl or a 4-cup sealable container. If desired, garnish with onions and cilantro. When serving, sprinkle the cashew sauce over the top.

Vegan Coconut Chickpea Curry

Preparation Time: 25 min

Serving: 4

INGREDIENTS

- 1 zucchini, halved and sliced
- 15 oz. chickpeas drained and rinsed
- 2 tsp. avocado oil
- 1 cup chopped onion
- ½ cup vegetable broth
- 4 cups baby spinach
- 2 cups precooked brown rice
- 1 cup diced bell pepper
- 1 ½ cups coconut curry simmer sauce

DIRECTIONS

1. Heat oil in a large-size skillet over medium-high heat. Add onion, pepper, and zucchini; cook, often stirring, until the vegetables begin to brown, 5 to 6 minutes.
2. Bring chickpeas, simmer sauce, and broth to a simmer, stirring constantly. Reduce to a standard-low heat and continue cooking until the vegetables are soft about 4 to 6 minutes. Just before serving, stir in spinach. Serve alongside rice.

Vegan Cauliflower Fried Rice

Preparation Time: 25 min

Serving: 4

INGREDIENTS

- 1 tsp. toasted sesame oil
- 1 tbsp. grated fresh ginger
- 1 tbsp. minced garlic
- ½ cup diced red bell pepper
- 3 tbsp. peanut oil, divided
- 3 scallions, sliced
- 1 cup frozen shelled edamame, thawed
- 4 cups riced cauliflower
- ⅓ cup unsalted roasted cashews
- 3 tbsp. soy sauce
- 1 cup trimmed and halved snow peas
- 1 cup shredded carrots

DIRECTIONS

1. Heat 1 tbsp peanut oil in a large-size wok or skillet over high heat. Add scallions, ginger, and garlic; cook, stirring, until scallions have softened, 30 to 40 seconds. Add bell pepper, snow peas, carrots, and edamame; cook, stirring, until just tender, 2 to 4 minutes. Transfer everything to a plate.
2. Add the prevailing 2 tbsp of peanut oil to the pan. Add cauliflower and stir until mostly softened about 2 minutes. Return the cooked vegetables to the pan, along with cashews, tamari (or soy sauce), and sesame oil. Stir until well combined.

Linguine with avocado, tomato & lime

Preparation Time: 32 min

Serving: 2

INGREDIENTS

- 115g wholemeal linguine
- 2 ripe tomatoes, chopped
- ½ pack fresh coriander, chopped
- 1 red onion, chopped
- 1 lime, zested and juiced
- 1 avocado, stoned, peeled, and chopped
- 1 red chili, deseeded and chopped, optional

DIRECTIONS

1. Cook the pasta according to pack instructions – about 10 mins. Meanwhile, put the lime juice and zest in a medium bowl with the avocado, tomatoes, coriander, onion, and chili, if using, and mix well.
2. Drain the pasta, toss it into the bowl and mix well. Serve straight away while still warm or cold.

Vegan sheet pan curried tofu & veggies

Preparation Time: 25 min

Serving: 3

INGREDIENTS

- 300 g firm tofu
- 300 g red peppers
- 40 g shallots
- 3 tbsp. olive oil
- 2 tsp. ground turmeric
- 2 tsp. garam masala
- 1/3 tsp medium chili powder
- a pinch of salt
- a bit of black pepper

DIRECTIONS

1. Tofu should be cut into tiny pieces and combined with 2 tablespoons of olive oil and seasonings.
2. All veggies should be cut and placed in a baking pan, followed by the tofu.
3. Bake for 10 minutes at 190°C in a preheated oven. Take the pan out of the range, mix, and bake for an additional 10 minutes. Cook for an extra minute if you want the tofu to get a little crispier. When ready, drizzle 1 tablespoon olive oil over the top and season with a sprinkle of black pepper.
4. Optional: just before serving, sprinkle 1 tablespoon parsley and a few slices of fresh red and green chilies on top. Although toppings are optional, they enhance the overall flavor of the dish.

Vegan tofu salad with sesame dressing

Preparation Time: 35 min

Serving: 1

182

INGREDIENTS

- Approx. 80 g mixed salad leaves
- 1 1/2 tsp freshly grated ginger
- 2 tsp sesame seeds
- a pinch of black pepper
- 1 tbsp. toasted sesame oil
- 1 medium-sized green bell pepper
- 170 g plain tofu
- 1 tbsp. + 2 tsp soy sauce
- 1 tbsp. extra virgin olive oil

DIRECTIONS

1. To prepare the marinated tofu, combine 1 tablespoon soy sauce and 1 tablespoon olive oil with the tofu (chopped into small cubes). Refrigerate the tofu for at least 20 minutes (or up to 4 hours) before cooking. If you're pressed for time, you can skip this step and simply combine the tofu with the remaining ingredients and cook it immediately.
2. Cook the tofu in a prepared non-stick pan or oven at 180°C until golden on the exterior and firm and nearly crispy inside. Allow for cooling before adding the tofu to the salad.
3. Salad: Combine the mixed leaves and finely chopped pepper in a bowl.
4. Combine the freshly grated ginger, 2 teaspoons soy sauce, 1 tablespoon toasted sesame oil, and 2 teaspoons sesame seeds in a small bowl.
5. Mix all elements in a bowl and season with a pinch of black pepper to taste. The dressing is added immediately before serving. If required, add additional sesame oil.

Zucchini Noodles with Avocado Sauce

Preparation Time: 20 min

Serving: 2

INGREDIENTS

- 1 zucchini
- 2 tbsp. lemon juice
- 1 avocado
- 1 1/4 cup basil
- 1/3 cup water
- 12 sliced cherry tomatoes
- 4 tbsp. pine nuts

DIRECTIONS

1. Use a peeler or the Spiralizer to create the zucchini noodles.
2. Blend the remaining ingredients (excluding the cherry tomatoes) until smooth in a blender.
3. Combine the noodles, avocado sauce, and cherry tomatoes in a mixing bowl.
4. Although these zucchini noodles with avocado sauce are best served fresh, they may be stored in the refrigerator for two days.

Middle Eastern Tabbouleh

Preparation Time: 20 min

Serving: 6

INGREDIENTS

- ½ cup extra-virgin olive oil
- ¼ cup lemon juice
- ½ tsp gray sea salt
- 2 bunches of fresh parsley, chopped
- 1 1/3 cup Manitoba Harvest Hemp Hearts
- 3 medium tomatoes, diced
- 1 small garlic clove, minced
- 8 green onions, finely diced
- 1/4 cup chopped fresh mint

DIRECTIONS

1. Mix the olive oil, lemon juice, and sea salt in a big pot. Combine with a whisk.
2. Toss in remaining ingredients and serve.

Vegan One-Pot Bean Chili

Preparation Time: 2 hr 10 min

Serving: 4

INGREDIENTS

- 1 cup Sun Ridge Farms Organic Chili Colorado + 4 cups water
- Salt and pepper
- 1 onion chopped
- 15 oz. diced tomatoes
- 1 ½ tbsp. Chili powder
- ½ tbsp. paprika
- 2 garlic cloves, minced
- 1 yellow bell pepper, chopped
- 3 tbsp. plus 4 cups water
- ¼ tsp. sea salt
- Dash of cayenne

DIRECTIONS

1. Bring the chili bean mixture and 4 cups water to a boil in a big pot. Once the water has been boiling, switch off the heat and allow the beans to soak for one hour.
2. Fill a colander halfway with beans. Rinse and drain well. Add three tbsp of water to the pan and sauté onion, garlic, and bell pepper for 5 minutes over medium heat. If required, add additional water to prevent sticking.
3. Frequently stir. Bring to a boil, then soaked beans and remaining ingredients (excluding the optional garnish). Decrease to low heat and cook, covered, for 2 hours, or until the beans are completely softened.
4. Sometimes stir the mixture to prevent it from sticking. Note: After about 1 hour, taste the chili (very carefully!) to see whether more spices should be added and adjust the flavor appropriately.

Sweet Potato Pie

Preparation Time: 42 min

Serving: 6

INGREDIENTS

- Mashed Sweet Potatoes
- 2 lb. Potatoes, peeled
- Salt and pepper to taste
- Veggie Layer
- 2 carrots - peeled and chopped
- ½ tsp. vegan Worcestershire sauce
- Pepper to taste
- Salt to taste
- 4 tbsp. vegetable stock
- 1 cup dry, brown lentils
- ½ tbsp. soy sauce
- 1 tsp. garlic powder
- 1 tsp. onion powder
- 3 cups water
- ¾ Cup frozen corn
- ¾ cup peas, frozen

DIRECTIONS

1. Peeled sweet potatoes should be halved lengthwise and then cut into pieces approximately 1 inch thick.
2. Place the sweet potato slices in a big saucepan and cover approximately 1-2 inches of water. Lead to a boil, lower to low heat, and continue cooking till fork-tender (10 mins.) Drain.
3. Mash the sweet potatoes with a fork or potato masher; season with salt and pepper. While the potatoes are cooking, sauté the carrots in a medium-sized saucepan with vegetable stock. Combine lentils and water in a medium bowl.
4. Lead to a boil and then reduce to low heat and continue cooking for 15 minutes, or until just tender. Cook for additional 5 minutes, stirring in the peas and corn. Garlic powder, Soy sauce, onion powder, and vegan Worcestershire sauce are used to season the lentil mixture.
5. Spice to taste with freshly ground pepper and salt. Preheat oven to 425 degrees Fahrenheit. In a 3-quart casserole dish, evenly distribute the lentils. Spread the mashed sweet potatoes equally on top, and leave for 15 minutes in the oven.

Beefless Stew

Preparation Time: 45 min

Serving: 6

192

INGREDIENTS

- 1 yellow Onion cut into sliced
- 2 cups low-sodium vegetable broth
- ½ cup water
- 6 garlic cloves, minced
- 3 stalks celery
- 2 cups frozen peas thawed
- ½ 6 oz. can tomato paste mixed plus water to thin
- 3 carrots
- 16 oz. mushrooms
- 2 lb. potatoes
- 1 tbsp. Italian herbs
- 1 tbsp. fresh rosemary chopped
- ½ tsp. smoked paprika

DIRECTIONS

1. Saute carrots, onion, and celery for a few minutes in a big soup pot with ¼ cup water. Continue sautéing for 1-2 minutes more with the garlic and mushroom.
2. Season with salt and pepper. Combine the vegetable broth, potatoes, tomato paste, herbs, smoked paprika, and herbs.
3. Cook wrapped over standard heat for about 20 minutes, or until the potatoes and carrots are soft. If the swelter is too thick, thin it with up to 1/2 cup water or as needed.
4. Blend about 1½ cups of the broth with a few veggies until smooth in a blender.
5. Stir the blended sauce back into the saucepan to mix. Add the frozen peas and cook for about 5 minutes. With crusty salad and bread, this dish makes a full dinner.

Broccoli, Red Pepper & Tofu Stir Fry

Preparation Time: 25 min

Serving: 2

194

INGREDIENTS

- ½ block extra firm tofu, cubed
- 4 cups broccoli
- 1 red bell pepper

For the sauce:

- 1-½ tbsp. Nutritional yeast
- ¼ tsp. Onion powder
- ¼ tsp. turmeric
- 1 cup water
- 1 ½ Tbsp. Low sodium soy sauce
- ¼ tsp. garlic powder

DIRECTIONS

1. To drain the tofu, wrap it on a paper towel. Allow tofu to drain for approximately 15-20 minutes.
2. While the tofu drains, mix the sauce ingredients in a small dish.
3. Bring to a boil in a big skillet. Cook broccoli over high heat until bright green. Cook until the broccoli gets a dark green color and the sauce has nearly disappeared.

Homefries

Preparation Time: 25 min

Serving: 4

- 3 tbsp. peanut butter
- Salt and pepper to taste
- 3 russet potatoes, cubed

DIRECTIONS

1. With cold water, rinse the potato cubes well. Then, drain them well. It's best to melt butter or margarine in a large pan over medium-low heat. Place the potatoes in the skillet, and stir them to coat them with butter. Salt and pepper your food. Cook for 10 minutes with a lid, then remove the cover and serve. In about 10 minutes, take off the top and keep turning the meat. It should be browned and crispy on all sides.

Rosemary red Skin potatoes

Preparation Time: 55 min

Serving: 4

INGREDIENTS

- 3 tbsp. extra-virgin olive oil
- 1 ½ lb. potatoes, cut into pieces
- 1 tbsp. chopped fresh rosemary
- Salt and ground black pepper to taste
- 2 tbsp. vegan cheese

DIRECTIONS

1. Preheat oven range to 425 degrees F (220 degrees C). Line a baking sheet with aluminum foil.
2. Mix potatoes, olive oil, cheese, and rosemary in a bowl. Season with salt and pepper. Spread potato mixture over the prepared baking sheet.
3. Bake in preheated oven until potatoes are golden brown and tender, stirring once, about 40 minutes.

Vegan Cheesy Crackers

Preparation Time: 45 min

Serving: 20

INGREDIENTS

- ½ cup almond flour
- ½ tsp. Baking powder
- ½ cup oat flour
- ½ tsp. Dried oregano, crushed
- 1 cup brown rice flour, + extra for sprinkling
- ½ cup + 2 tbsp. unsweetened, coconut milk
- 1 tbsp. tahini
- 1 tbsp. miso paste
- 1 tsp. Lemon juice
- ½ cup chickpea flour
- ½ tsp. Garlic powder
- ½ tsp. Onion powder
- ½ tsp. paprika

DIRECTIONS

1. Preheat oven to 325 degrees Fahrenheit. Preheat oven to 350°F. Line two baking pans with parchment paper. Combine the first nine ingredients in a large-size mixing bowl (through oregano).
2. Combine miso paste, milk, tahini, and lemon juice in a small blender. Cover and mix at high speed until smooth. Combine milk mixture and flour mixture; lightly knead to form a dough. Divide dough in half and form each half into a brick.
3. Put a silicone baking mat on a clean work area and lightly dust it with rice flour. Place 1 brick of dough on the mat and roll it into an even 1/16-inch-thick rectangle using a rolling pin. With a fork, poke the rectangle many times.
4. Cut the rectangle into 2-inch squares using a 2-inch square cookie cutter (or a pizza cutter, bench scraper, or long knife). Move the squares to one of the baking sheets that have been prepared.
5. Continue with the second dough brick and baking sheet, adding residual dough scraps.
6. Bake for 20 minutes, or until crackers are lightly browned, changing baking sheets halfway through the baking time. Allow crackers to cool completely on wire racks before serving. To keep hackers fresh, store them in a resealable plastic bag at room temperature for up to 10 days.

Vegan meringues

Preparation Time: 1 hr 43 min

Serving: 12

INGREDIENTS

- 100g golden caster sugar
- 400g chickpeas
- Soya cream and fruit, optional

DIRECTIONS

1. Preheat oven to 110°C/90°C fan/gas 14 and line a baking sheet with parchment paper. Over a bowl, drain the can of chickpeas, reserving the chickpeas for another purpose.
2. Read the chickpea water until soft peaks form (similar to egg whites using an electric mixer). Add the sugar gradually, frequently whisking, until the mixture is thick and glossy. This stage is critical for the meringues to retain their shape, and you'll whisk for up to 10 minutes - significantly longer than you would for a typical meringue.
3. Spoon or pipe the meringue mixture in 8cm blobs over the tray. Bake for 1 hour and 15 minutes, or until the crust is crunchy. Allow cooling slightly before topping with soya cream and fruit if used.

Lime, Sesame & Coconut Courgette Carpaccio

Preparation Time: 20 min

Serving: 4

INGREDIENTS

- 2 tbsp. sesame oil
- 150g mixed radishes, cut into wedges
- 3 tbsp. flaked coconut, toasted
- 1 lime juice
- 100g frozen shelled edamame beans
- 3 courgettes, spiralized into thin noodles

DIRECTIONS

1. Set a small saucepan of salted water to a boil. Drop in the edamame beans and cook for 3–4 mins, then using a slotted spoon, plunge into a bowl of ice-cold water. Once completely cool, tip into a sieve and leave to drain.
2. Mix the sesame oil with the lime juice in a small bowl with sea salt. Lay the courgette ribbons on a sharing platter. Scatter over the mixed radishes and edamame beans, then drizzle over the dressing and top with the toasted coconut.